Gwrello Glaw
Let it rain

by **Tanya Brittain**

Original poems in Cornish and English language

By the same author

Cornish by Design

Published in the UK by
Trelawny's Reach 2019
trelawnysreach.com
publishing@trelawnysreach.com

For

Carmen

CONTENTS

INTRODUCTION

Kernewek, the Cornish language, makes Cornwall distinctly different. Although the number of new speakers has grown rapidly in recent years, there are only around five thousand people able to speak it.

Language is part of Cornwall's heritage and unique cultural identity and Cornish is a recognised minority language under the European Charter for Regional or Minority Languages. Along with Welsh and Breton, Cornish is descended directly from the Common Brittonic language spoken throughout much of Britain before the English language came to dominate.

Cornish was in common use in Cornwall until the late 18th century and was spoken widely 'in the home' well into the latter part of the 19th century. A revival began in the early 20th century, championed by Celtic language scholar, Henry Jenner. Cornish now has a growing number of second-language speakers. It is being taught in schools again and a small number of people in Cornwall have been raised as bilingual native speakers.

Author, Tanya Brittain, describes herself as a cultural ambassador and Cornish language student. Tanya has made an outstanding contribution to the promotion of Cornwall's traditional culture, heritage and language over the past decade.

Tanya has commissioned and produced many live performances, short films and vox pops featuring famous faces speaking or singing in Cornish. The Artistic Director of a large music festival for over five years, Tanya was responsible for several projects involving the creation of new music in both English and Cornish language, including the Big Cornish Sing – a live broadcast which took place in 2017 attracting a digital reach of almost two million viewers worldwide.

An award-winning writer, songwriter and touring musician, Tanya formed folk band, The Changing Room, with vocalist Sam Kelly in 2014. Her original music in Cornish language has been broadcast live on BBC Radio 4, BBC Radio 3 and BBC Radio 2. The Changing Room's debut album, *Behind the Lace,* is listed in *The Telegraph's* 'Best Folk albums of 2015'.

Tanya has been writing a monthly bilingual column for international culture and lifestyle magazine *Cornwall Today* for over two years and is the author of the bilingual book, *Cornish by Design*. This poetry book is a collection of Tanya's original song lyrics in English language, with Cornish translations provided by linguist Ken George.

Ever wondered what the Cornish language sounds like? Search '**Gwrello Glaw by The Changing Room**' online and find out – over a million people already have.

Gwrello Glaw

Let it rain

GENEV DONS

Prys yw gyllys pell
Ow hunros 'wren
Y tova dhymm ha'm kara
Ruvanes par dell ven
Mes tremen hir an termyn
Ny vern dhymmo-vy
Pana drajedi!

Avod mes a'm penn
Nyns a tra yn-rag
Naswedhow an klokk hogen yth yns stag
Kildenn dhe'th le teythi
Re gyffi jy hwyth
Yn ifarn leski bydh

Genev dons
Travyth ny hevel bones gwir
Genev dons
Hunros terrys yw ow hastell dir
Dehwelydh hwath yn-bann
Avel goedhanes tro an tan
Ha kudhys dha skilys kyn fons
Genev dons

Kolonn drogh
A wodhevydh hy fayn?
Pan ro tenkys y hwaff
'Yll'ta dyghtya an payn?
Gas vy dhe'th weles, mar pleg
A wrug an bywnans dha vos gwrekk?

Avod mes a'm gols
Ke-jy yn kerdh
Mir mes na dav
Hy holonn dinerth
Kildenn dhe'th le teythi
Dha hunros a vydh
Yn ifarn leskys bydh

Eus tenkys fella y'n bys oll
Es gwruthyl gortos ow folyers foll
Ow kroghen velynhes heb howl
Hebdho yw drog dowl
Avod mes a'm chi, an gwari yw bras
Poket dre hanow ha Poket dre nas
Kildenn dhe'th le teythi
Ow sians a vydh
Yn ifarn leski bydh

DANCE WITH ME

Once upon a time
I dared to dream
He came to me and loved me
As if I was a queen
Now days and weeks and years
Mean nothing to me
Such a tragedy!

Get out of my head
Nothing has changed
Not even the hands on the clock rearrange
Get back where you came from
I bid you farewell
I hope you burn in hell

Dance with me
Nothing's ever quite what it seems
Dance with me
In the castle of my broken dreams
Like moths around a flame
You just keep coming back again
Whatever your motive may be
Dance with me

Do you know
How broken heart feels?
Could you handle the pain
And the hand that fate deals?
Let me look at you now if I may
And all that life has worn away

Get out of my hair
Go off and play
Look but don't touch
Her heart will betray
Go back where you came from
I bid you farewell
Your dreams can burn in hell

Could there be a crueler fate
Than to make my baying public wait
No sun upon my yellow skin whilst I'm without him
Get out of my house, it's all just a game
Pocket by nature and Pocket by name
Go back where you came from
I bid you farewell
I'd rather burn in hell

DOWN YN-DANN AN MOR

Ow horf yth yw kogh leska, war vor yma ow chi
Ow soedh yth yw pyskessa, ow spyrys y'ga thri
An goelyow leun a awel, an warak vras a nev
War dhowr yma ow holonn, goelanes pell a lev

An mor a wra dha vaga, ha'th bywnans ev a berth
Dha sevel, dha govia, po treghi gans y nerth
Dha vovya gans y alloes
Dha skoedhya pan vo res
Mes dibita 'hwra dha skonya
Ow gwarnyans yth yw gwrys

Pan vinhwertho, spavennhes
Dres eghenn uvel bydh
Dha lok a allo perthi
Ha'th gasa saw yn klor
Mar ny wrylli y enora
Fethesik ty a vydh
Y'th gorr-jy bys dha bowesva
Down yn-dann an mor

DEEP BENEATH THE SEA

My body is a lugger, my home is on the sea
My labour is in fishing, my spirit in all three
The fullness of the sailcloth, the vast unbroken sky
My heart lies on the water, where distant seagulls cry

She's the one who feeds you, the one who carries life
She can lift you and protect you, or cut you like a knife
She'll excite you with her power
And support you when in need
But she's ruthless and will shun you
My warning you should heed

When she smiles and all is calm
Show deep humility
She may tolerate your presence
And gently leave you be
But if you don't respect her
A victim you will be
She'll take you to your resting place
Deep beneath the sea

HENWYN ORTH FOS

'Th ens-i yo'nk, 'th ens-i fethus,
Ha kyns koedha, bywek ens
Y hwrens-i dever, tramor ha pell a-dre
Leun a woeth kevennyn, tru
Kyn dre vilyow 'th ens dhe'n lu
Y feuns kellys
Peub y honan yn y le

Agan gwer yth ens, ha'gan breder
Agan tasow, mebyon guv
Yth ens krev yn brys
Ha lymm yn-rag dhe vos
Mes yn korf sojetys ankow
Hag yn kolonn skwerdys ens
Yth ens hedorr, 'vel mylles war an ros

Y skrifen dhedha-i pup dydh
Lies tra ny gewsyn bydh
Mes y pysyn-ni *bydh saw, bydh krev, sa'bann'*
I a redya skriptor sans
Kyns a ifarn mos war-nans
'Ga henwyn ni a red orth fos a-vann

NAMES ON A WALL

They were young, they were handsome
They were vital when they fell
They did their duty, they were far away from home
We remember full of pride
And with sadness we confide
They joined in thousands
But they left the world alone

They were our husbands and our brothers
Our fathers and our sons
They were strong of mind
And keen to take command
But their bodies they were mortal
And their hearts were torn apart
They were fragile, like poppies in the sand

We wrote them letters everyday
So many things we didn't say
Instead, we prayed *'stay safe, be brave, stand tall'*
They read their bibles whilst in hell
Then they said their last farewell
And now we read their names on a wall

POWL PENNGELLI TRUAN

Powl Penngelli truan, pyskessa o y hwel
Unn avloes bras a wruga, ky'n jevo kolonn lel
Y truflas gans morvoren yn Baya Seythyn splann
Yn y wel hy dons, ha puptra eth dhe vann

Y'n myttin na dhe'n bora
Dhe vor an kokow eth
Yth esa'n hern ow hesa a-dhyghow hag a-gledh
Ha'n dus orth aga hachya
An voren hi a dheuth
Yn y wel hy dons
Kyn hwodhya ev an keudh

Pan veu an rosow kreunys, an voren y'ga mysk
A wynni ha batalyas krev
Keffrys ha lies pysk
Penngelli a's divaglas, a's livras gans y lown
Yn y wel hy dons, ha hi ow sedhi down
Mes y'n kablas rag hy hachya
Ha gorra hus y'n dre
Ha gans hy soen, y hwrug hi doen
An tewes yn pub le

Powl Penngelli truan, a'n roes y's dyllas ev
Mes Seythyn kleudhsa hi heb keudh
Kov may hwrello ev
Otta gwirder an gweylgi, y lagha a vydh
Voys dynyek an voren, ha reyth an re rydh

POOR OLD PAUL PENGELLY

Poor old Paul Pengelly, a fisherman by trade
His heart was pure and gentle, but one mistake he made
He flirted with a mermaid out in Seaton Bay
He watched her dance, it all went wrong that day

That morning, at the first light
The seine boats put to sea
Pilchard out there topping for all the world to see
And as the men were netting
The mermaid came to view
And he watched her dance
Although he knew he shouldn't do

As the nets were gathered, the mermaid she was caught
Along with twenty thousand fish
She struggled and she fought
Pengelly to her rescue, he cut the siren free
And he watched her dance as she swam back out to sea
But she cursed him for her capture
Put a hex upon the land
As she rolled, her spell took hold
And the town was deep in sand

Poor old Paul Pengelly, he freed her from the net
But she would drown old Seaton town
Lest he should forget
It's the way of the ocean, the code of the sea
The sound of the siren, the right of the free

ROEV SOS ROEV

"He'va, he'va", Brennyas
Kraf dha rosow, ke dhe'n mor
Aspi gluw war-tu ha'n garmer hag a-bell
Brennyas, gid dha dus
May fo roevys ewn a-brys
Gwith hi saw, syns hi kompes gans dha nell

Mis-Hedra 'teu dynsoges
Ha mis-Du herynnys gwynn
Tewedhow gwav 'an gwith ni war an tir
Kankres pals, brithylli splann
Der an gwenton ni a gan
Hag y'n withva gorryn hern y'n havas hir

Roev sos roev
Roev erbynn an fros, sos
Bo an Garmer hos, sos, roev
Roev sos roev
Y's kechyn ni yn syth sos
Roev bys pan vi skwith sos, roev

War an flour, kowellow gwag
An hes a way dhe'n est
Agan skathow 'denn an roes ha kylgh yw gwrys
An Garmer, ev a wra an desenn He'va da
Agan kok yw leun, 'gan krysyow glyb dre hwys

Mowysi mas a's gwra pur lan
Ha's bernya saw ha sygh
Talgellow leun a hoelan, skansow brav
Puptydh mires orth an mayn
Skwattys yns dhe ri an saym
Rag pesya der an gewer dhrog yn gwav

Yeghes da dhe dus Katholik
Re bo bywnans hir dhe'n Pab
Mayth ystynno ev Korawys dre hwegh mis
Rag y dus py le ny vern
Nyns eus travyth avel hern
Aga enev rag y selwel war an bys

ROW BOYS ROW

"Hevva, hevva", Bowsman
Grab your nets and put to sea
Keep an eye upon the Huer and the haze
Bowsman, guide your crew
Steer your oarsmen straight and true
Keep her safe, hold her steady as she sways

November brings the herring
And October brings the hake
The storms of winter keep us firm ashore
We'll be crabbing in the spring
Hauling mackerel as we sing
And in summer we put pilchard into store

Row boys row
Row against the tide boys
Hear the Huer cry boys, row
Row boys, row
We'll catch them on the run boys
Row until you're done boys, row

Empty baskets line the deck
The shoal is moving east
Our seine-boats form a circle with the net
The Huer's off to bake the welcome Hevva cake
Our load is full, our shirts are wet with sweat

The womenfolk will clean them all
And stack them high and dry
Our cellars fill with salt and silver scales
Then our daily toil
Will be to press them for the oil
To see us through the winter storms and gales

And then we'll drink the health of Catholic folk
And to the Pope
They can search the whole world over, pole to pole
May they all repent and extend their term of Lent
For there's nothing quite like pilchard
For the saving of the soul

YNTREDHA DOWR A RES

Gans an lanow y hwoelsyn hag entra y'n porth
Ha'n roesow o lenwys a hes
Unn dre orth an lewbordh hag onan a-borth
Hag yntredha, dowr a res
War an kay 'th esa hi gans hy hanstell y'n dorn
Ny welis vyth tekter somper
Hi war an lann west, ha my orth an est
Hag yntredhon, dowr a ver
Pan en dhe vor a'n le, hwath trigys ov yn de
Puptra a janjyas gans treylyans an fros
Toll-treth yw genev pes, arta yth en yn-mes
A'm serth vy rygdhi ny wrug lowr a dros
Rag yntredhon dowr a res

Gans growan y teuthons dhe sevel an pons
Defens na ragwelsens o krev
Unn dre gans an arghans, hy ben yn-dann Howl
Hag yntredha dowr a sev
Pan en dhe vor a'n le, hwath trigys ov yn de
Puptra a janjyas gans treylyans an fros
'Ma pell a-ughov vy, ow fries ny vydh hi
Pons ny dreyl tra, pan eus aswa re vros
Rag yntredhon dowr a res

Ha lemmyn 'ma troe'lergh a'n est bys y'n west
Ha mowes yw yowynk ha teg
Mes oesweyth a gas a dhiberth an dhiw dre
Hag yntredha dowr a freg

A RIVER RUNS BETWEEN

Into harbour we sailed on the incoming tide
Our fishing nets full of sardine
One town to the starboard and one to the port
And a river ran between
On the quayside, she stood with her basket in hand
Such beauty I've never since seen
But she on the west bank and me on the east
And a river ran between
And as we haul away, I'm still in yesterday
Everything changed with the turn of the tide
I paid the ferryman, anchors aweigh again
My love for her I did never confide
'Cos a river runs between

The bridge builders came with their Caradon stone
Resistance they hadn't foreseen
One town has the money, the other the sun
And a river runs between
And as we haul away, I'm still in yesterday
Everything changed with the turn of the tide
She's way above me, my bride she will never be
A bridge doesn't change things, the gap is too wide
And a river runs between

So now there's a path from the east to the west
And a pretty young maid of eighteen
But a lifetime of conflict the two towns divide
And a river runs between

OW GOES YMA Y'TH GLOW

Ow holonn yw 'vel growan
A'm spyrys kevsys prow
Ow horf-vy koth ka krommys
Ow goes yma y'th glow

Gorr vy bys dhe'n teudhji
Pan ylliv vy dhe goll
Y'm skevens yma kober pals
Mes y'm poket travyth oll
Ow holonn yw 'vel growan
A'm spyrys kevsys prow
Ow horf-vy koth ka krommys
Ow goes yma y'th glow

Den-bal yth o ow thas-vy
Y das an keth, devri
'Ma aga goes y'th glow, Syrra
Namoy ny balons-i
'Tho tyb orthiv y'n gwavas
Dha dan ow leski gluw
Rag yn-dann dhor y hweythav
Ow thremynn pup-prys du

Ow holonn yw 'vel growan
A'm spyrys kevsys prow
Ow horf-vy koth ka krommys
Ow goes yma y'th glow

Ha tyb orthiv y'n gwenton
Dha worhel pan dheu tre
Y benn a-rag a gober
Gans sten y hwrussys pe
Porth kov jy, war dha diryow
Pan splann an Howl yn hav
Y'n tewlder my a ober
Gans arsenek warnav

Ow holonn yw 'vel growan
A'm spyrys kevsys prow
Ow horf-vy koth ka krommys
Ow goes yma y'th glow

Ha tyb orthiv y'n kynyav
An Howl pan nes dhe'n min
Re spenis bywnans yn-dann dhor
'Tho spar vy orth ow fin
Ha gorr vy bys dhe'n teudhji
Pan ylliv vy dhe goll
Y'm skevens yma kober pals
Mes y'm poket travyth oll

Ow holonn yw 'vel growan
A'm spyrys kevsys prow
Ow horf-vy koth ka krommys
Ow goes yma y'th glow

MY BLOOD IS ON YOUR COAL

My heart it is like granite
My spirit you have sold
My body old and broken
My blood is on your coal

Take me to the smelter
When I'm dead and gone
For there's copper plenty in my lungs
But in my pocket, I have none
My heart it is like granite
My spirit you have sold
My body old and broken
My blood is on your coal

My father was a miner
And so was his before
Their blood is on your coal, Sir
They don't mine anymore
So, think of me in winter
When your fire burns bright
'Cos I'll be working underground
My face as black as night

My heart it is like granite
My spirit you have sold
My body old and broken
My blood is on your coal

And think of me in springtime
When your ship comes in
'Cos her bow is lined with copper
And you paid for her with tin
And in the heart of summer
When sun shines on your land
I'll be working in the darkness
With arsenic on my hands

My heart it is like granite
My spirit you have sold
My body old and broken
My blood is on your coal

And give a thought in autumn
As sun sets in the sky
I've spent my life beneath the earth
So spare me when I die
And take me to the smelter
When I'm dead and gone
For there's copper plenty in my lungs
But in my pocket, I have none

My heart it is like granite
My spirit you have sold
My body old and broken
My blood is on your coal

GWRELLO GLAW

Saw vy, a'n vorladron yn ow brys
Na wrellons i ow fetha
Na'm dallo tewlder 'n bys
Gwith vy, a'n tewolgow down y'n nos
Le may tin an levow enos

Kudh vy, ha'n dewolow oll a-dro
ha tenn vy tro ha'n sawder
koedh gansa ma na vo
Gid vy, bydh ow lugarn, bydh ow sos
Bydh y'n kommol an toll
Dredho howl ow tos

Gwrello glaw, 'wrello glaw
A wel an min y hyllis dos yn saw
Gwrello bras, 'wrello sorr
Dons a wrav, dones war neb kor

Kach vy, mar tallethis mos dhe'n senn
Pan dro dhe wav an kynyav
Ha ny dheu dhymm howl nahen
Syns vy, ha bydh na'm gas dhe vos
Gwith vy saw bys gwenton

Gwrello glaw, 'wrello glaw
A wel an min y hyllis dos yn saw
Gwrello bras, 'wrello sorr
Dons a wrav, dones war neb kor

LET IT RAIN

Save me, from the pirates of my mind
Don't let them overcome me
Don't let the darkness blind
Keep me, from the shadows of the night
Where the voices call you onward

Hide me, as the demons gather 'round
And drag me back to safety
Don't let them take me down
Guide me, be my searchlight, be my crew
Be the hole in the cloud
Where the sun breaks through

Let it rain, let it rain
'Cos I've seen the edge and made it back again
Let it rage, let it pour
I will dance, I'll be back for more

Catch me, if the downturn has begun
As autumn turns to winter
And I'm sheltered from the sun
Hold me, and don't every let me go
And keep me safe 'til springtime

Let it rain, let it rain
'Cos I've seen the edge and made it back again
Let it rage, let it pour
I will dance, I'll be back for more

HAL-AN-TOW

Losow hav yw pynnys
Orth mowysi teg
Rudh rosennow y'ga bogh
Garlontow hir a greg
Gwesyon y'ga hattow brav
Keffrys eskyjyow splann
Prys dhe be kendonow oll
May fo an reken glan

Ow ri dorn dhe oll an bys
Kothmens dha, envi
Fin an gwavas, gwren ni vri
An vlydhen goth yw gyllys glan
Dhe'n nowydh dynnargh ri
Y tonsyav kyns, ha gul ow hyns
A-dreus an plen dhywgh hwi

Trev ha pow yn hal-an-tow
Gans dons ha boes ha lev
Trev ha pow y'n hal-an-tow
Dhe'n gwenton ni a ev

Kler ha splann an korev
Rudh ha gwynn an ros
An sols y'th yalgh, a Syrra hweg
A bleksa dhymm, re'm fydh
An eth mis-Me, an gwav yw de
Goel Vighal ev a vydh

An glaswas rag gwelsowas
A led an donsyow sarf
Tus, benynes, yo'nk ha loes
An devos a yn skarf
An dons rag bywnans, dons rag howl
Ha dons rag aventur

Gonisyn has ha'n drevas a vydh sur
An vlydhen goth yw gyllys glan
Dhe'n nowydh dynnargh ri
Y tonsyav kyns, ha gul ow hyns
A-dreus an plen dhywgh hwi

Trev ha pow yn hal-an-tow
Gans dons ha boes ha lev
Trev ha pow y'n hal-an-tow
Dhe'n gwenton ni a ev

HAL-AN-TOW

Lily of the valley
Pinned to maidens fair
The red of roses in their cheeks
And garlands in their hair
Menfolk in their finery
All hats and polished shoes
Time to settle all their debts
And pay what's overdue

Shaking hands with 'one and all'
Enemies and friends
We'll see the old year out in style
And welcome in the new
I'll dance and sway
And weave my way
Across the square to you

And a-way we go with the hal-an-tow
We'll dance and feast and sing
A-way we go with the hal-an-tow
We'll drink and toast the spring

Rose and white the roses
Clear and bright the ale
A shilling in your purse kind Sir
I wish that it were mine
The eighth of May, Saint Michael's Day
The end of wintertime

The green man brings fertility
And leads the serpentine
Men and women, young and old
Our rituals combine
We dance for new life, dance for sun
And dance for fortunes fair

We sow our seed and a harvest we prepare
We'll see the old year out in style
And welcome in the new
I'll dance and sway and weave my way
Across the square to you

And a-way we go with the hal-an-tow
We'll dance and feast and sing
A-way we go with the hal-an-tow
We'll drink and toast the spring

Thanks

Ken George – who has translated my poetry and song lyrics into Kernewek since 2014.

Paul Greenwood – for hours of inspirational stories about Cornwall's fishing heritage and for the gift of a beautiful, old, Cornish dictionary.

Carmen Hunt – who unwittingly instigated my love affair with Cornish language.

Special thanks

Gareth Rhys Jones, for his love and encouragement, as always.

P&M, for giving me the space to by myself, as well as their mother.

Finally, thanks to all the people who have told me 'no' in life. You know who you are. You have been a constant source of motivation.

About the author

Tanya Brittain describes herself as a cultural ambassador, Cornish language student, writer and tea drinker. Tanya has Breton ancestry but was born and raised in South Yorkshire, England. She graduated from Art college in the 80s and her first job was in the mining industry as an illustrator of specialist equipment for technical publications. She progressed rapidly through the ranks into general management and marketing. Working in the publishing, food and music industries over a period of twenty years, she ended up in Cornwall working on a six-month project. Six months became six years, six years became twelve, etc.

Working actively with other Celtic nations and connecting with Cornish diaspora worldwide, Tanya has made an outstanding contribution to the promotion of Cornwall's traditional culture, heritage and language over the past decade.

An award-winning writer, songwriter and touring musician, Tanya formed folk band, **The Changing Room**, with vocalist Sam Kelly in 2014. Her original music in Cornish language has been broadcast live on BBC Radio 4, BBC Radio 3 and BBC Radio 2 and recordings by The Changing Room are afforded regular airplay worldwide. The Changing Room's debut album is listed in *The Telegraph's* 'Best Folk albums of 2015'. Tanya has commissioned and produced many live performances, short films and vox pops featuring famous faces speaking or singing in Cornish. The Artistic Director of a large music festival for over five years, Tanya was responsible for designing and delivering several projects involving the creation of new music in both English and Cornish language, including the Big Cornish Sing – a live broadcast which attracted a digital reach of almost two million viewers.

Tanya has written a monthly bilingual column for international culture and lifestyle magazine *Cornwall Today* for over two years, and has published a compilation of bilingual short stories under the title **Cornish by Design**. This is her first bilingual poetry book.

www.ingramcontent.com/pod-product-compliance
Lightning Source LLC
Chambersburg PA
CBHW050046040726
47599CB00015B/1828